Kipper's Alphabet I Spy

Written by Kate Ruttle and Annemarie Young,
based on original characters created by Roderick Hunt and Alex Brychta
Illustrated by Alex Brychta

OXFORD
UNIVERSITY PRESS

I spy with my little eye, something beginning with...

apple, ant, Biff, banana, ball, cat, candle

4

dinosaur, duck, egg, elephant, Floppy, feather

goose, goat, gate, hair, hat, horse, insect

j

k

l

jelly, jigsaw, Kipper, key, kangaroo, ladybird, lion

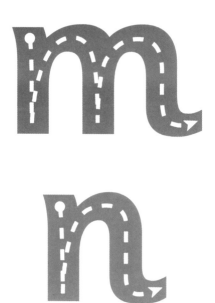

moon, monkey, milk, nose, nail, net

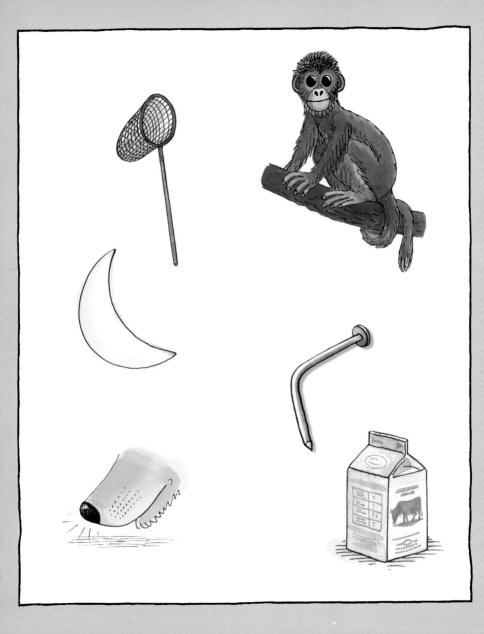

orange, octopus, pear, penguin, purple, queen, quilt

red, rabbit, rainbow, sandwich, sun, tiger, teddy, t-shirt

umbrella, under, volcano, violin, watermelon, watch

18

fox, box, yellow, yo-yo, yawn, zebra, zigzag

A maze

Help Kipper get to Floppy.